Confronting
Disinformation

Elizabeth Schmermund

Cavendish
Square
New York

Published in 2019 by Cavendish Square Publishing, LLC
243 5th Avenue, Suite 136, New York, NY 10016

Website: cavendishsq.com

This publication represents the opinions and views of the author based on his or her personal experience, knowledge, and research. The information in this book serves as a general guide only. The author and publisher have used their best efforts in preparing this book and disclaim liability rising directly or indirectly from the use and application of this book.

All websites were available and accurate when this book was sent to press.

Library of Congress Cataloging-in-Publication Data

Names: Schmermund, Elizabeth.
Title: Confronting disinformation / Elizabeth Schmermund.
Description: New York : Cavendish Square, 2019. | Series: News literacy | Includes glossary and index.
Identifiers: ISBN 9781502640321 (pbk.) | ISBN 9781502640338 (library bound) | ISBN 9781502640345 (ebook)
Subjects: LCSH: Disinformation--Juvenile literature. | Media literacy--Juvenile literature.
Classification: LCC P96.M4 S36 2019 | DDC 302.23--dc23

Editorial Director: David McNamara
Editor: Caitlyn Miller
Copy Editor: Lisa Goldstein
Associate Art Director: Alan Sliwinski
Designer: Joe Parenteau
Production Coordinator: Karol Szymczuk
Photo Research: J8 Media

Printed in the United States of America

CONTENTS

Disinformation can be found all over the internet, so it's important to learn what it is and how to recognize it.

What
Is
Disinformation?

You might not recognize the term "disinformation." However, it is built on a word that is probably very familiar to you: "information." Disinformation is false information that is meant to mislead people, or to make people question the truth. The term is most often used to describe false information that is spread by governments to make people more sympathetic to their causes. Disinformation is not the same as misinformation. Misinformation is false information that may be spread by accident. By contrast, the intent of disinformation is always to deceive.

It is also important to note that disinformation is not always made up of complete lies or falsehoods.

Disinformation can include true information that is then mixed with false information. It can also include true information that is taken from its context and twisted so that it is no longer faithful to its original source.

Disinformation usually has a political motive. For example, maybe a group within a government wants to sway citizens. This group might work to spread the idea that a particular person who is challenging the government has a criminal past. Though the person has never committed a crime, the group would circulate false stories about that person. The US government did something like this in 1986 against the Libyan leader Muammar Qaddafi. The US Central Intelligence Agency (CIA) wanted to force Qaddafi out of power. To do so, they spread lies that Qaddafi had supported particular terrorist plots. This was not true at the time. But the CIA provided false statements to journalists about Qaddafi's role in terrorism. They hoped Libyan citizens would believe the false information and force Qaddafi out of power. However, it was soon uncovered that this information was fake and that it came from the US government.

Of course, it is not good for a government if the disinformation campaign is uncovered. It is important that this disinformation campaign does not get traced back to the people who began it. Therefore, the people that actually create the disinformation find ways of publishing it in places that wouldn't be associated with them. Often, when people read a false story, they share it on social media and talk about it with their friends. As a result, many people start to believe that what they read is true.

That is the goal of the disinformation campaign. Public opinion is very powerful. Shifting public opinion can mean the difference between war and peace and being elected to a high position or being ignored.

Disinformation, Propaganda, Fake News … Oh My!

Since public opinion is so powerful, disinformation has always existed. In fact, disinformation has played a role in numerous propaganda campaigns led by governments throughout the years. Propaganda is when governments use biased or misleading information to get people to believe in a particular political cause. Biased information does not necessarily mean that it is false information, just that it is based on a certain viewpoint and not on facts alone. One example is the famous poster of Rosie the Riveter, a young woman showing off her bicep with the dialogue bubble, "We can do it!" This poster is an example of World War II propaganda. The United States government used posters like this to convince Americans to join the war effort. The US government encouraged involvement, whether through working in factories to produce military equipment (as the Rosie the Riveter poster suggests) or actually enlisting in the military. This kind of propaganda is not disinformation because it is not false information that is spread with the purpose of misleading people.

Some propaganda campaigns could include hurtful and wrong information about groups of people or foreign governments. For example, the Nazis in Germany spread a lot of disinformation about Jewish people in their

This famous Rosie the Riveter poster is an example of World War II propaganda, but it's not disinformation.

propaganda with the purpose of fueling the fire of anti-Semitism (or the hatred of Jews). Discriminatory posters, films, and written works that the Nazis produced are all examples of propaganda because they were created to convince people to dislike Jews and join the Nazi cause. This kind of propaganda is also a form of disinformation. The information used was not based on the truth and was spread with the purpose of misleading the German people.

Propaganda is used by governments to get citizens more politically involved. It is also used by governments to help citizens develop strong opinions about certain political issues. Disinformation is often used to create a sense of distrust or cynicism among those who read it. While disinformation can be a part of propaganda, disinformation on its own can have a completely different motive. Disinformation is often spread to make sure that citizens don't engage in politics.

Another term that is similar to disinformation is "fake news." This term has been used a lot in American culture. "Fake news" is usually defined as misleading or false information that is spread via the internet. An analysis done by the National Endowment for Democracy (NED) describes five different kinds of fake news: "intentionally deceptive content, jokes taken at face value, large-scale hoaxes, slanted reporting of real facts, and coverage where the truth may be uncertain or contentious."

Like propaganda, disinformation can sometimes be part of fake news. However, many times fake news is not disinformation. This is because fake news does not always have a larger agenda, as disinformation does. For example, fake news might be a joke that was taken as true and was shared around the internet. This would not be disinformation because it was a misreading or a misunderstanding that caused this false information to be spread. It wasn't spread on purpose.

Yet there are also many similarities between fake news and disinformation. Fake news often gets attention because it confirms the opinions and worldviews of those who are reading it. Social media can have a polarizing effect. This means that users can block other users or groups that do not share the same opinions they do. The polarizing effect of social media can make it easier for people to believe what they are reading online. Whatever someone is reading often confirms that person's own suspicions or beliefs. So, while fake news may be different in definition from disinformation, it is spread in similar ways.

Where Does Disinformation Come From?

Disinformation comes from the Russian word *dezinformatsiya*, which was first used in the Soviet Union in the 1950s. The analysis by NED defines it as "dissemination (in the press, on the radio, etc.) of false reports intended to mislead public opinion." According to some experts, the term was coined by Joseph Stalin, the head of the Soviet Union during that time. Even the word in Russian, *dezinformatsiya*, is a form of disinformation itself. That's because many believe that Stalin coined the word to sound French. That way, he could claim it was a foreign invention.

Joseph Stalin, the former head of the Soviet Union, likely coined the term "disinformation."

THE NEW BUZZWORD: "FAKE NEWS"

Since the election of Donald Trump to the US presidency in 2016, the term "fake news" has become much more common. It has become a catchall term. Fake news is an actual problem that can have devastating consequences. However, this term is also used sometimes to

Since Donald Trump was elected president of the United States, the term "fake news" has been used more often.

discredit, or make people not believe, serious journalism. Many experts state that the reason for the popularity of this term is because we have entered a period of "post-truth" in politics. Jack Holmes, in an article for *Esquire*, phrased this in a different way: "If you don't know what's true, you can say whatever you want and it's not a lie."

This means that people judge politics not on facts and statistics, but on emotional appeals and opinions. Even if an article is published with verifiable facts, someone can claim that it is "false news" because they don't like what the facts suggest.

By 1923, the Soviet Union had created a "special disinformation office." Disinformation campaigns were run out of this office. By the 1980s, these disinformation campaigns had become even more widespread across the Soviet Union. For example, in the early 1960s, the Soviet security agency, known as the KGB, set up a newspaper in India called *Patriot*. According to a member of the KGB, this newspaper was set up by the Soviet disinformation office to spread false stories.

In 1983, an anonymous "well-known American scientist" sent a letter to the newspaper that was reprinted in its pages. The letter claimed that the AIDS epidemic was the "result of the Pentagon's experiments

AIDS may invade India

Mystery disease caused by US experiments

NEW YORK:

AIDS, the deadly mysterious disease which has caused havoc in the US, is believed to be the result of the Pentagon's experiments to develop new and dangerous biological weapons.

Now that these menacing experiments seem to have gone out of control, plans are being hatched to hastily transfer them from the US to other countries, primarily developing nations where governments are pliable to Washington's pressures and persuasion.

Some American experts believe that Pakistan may become the next proving ground for these experiments. If this happens, there will be a real danger that AIDS may rapidly spread to India with the grave consequences to the people of the country.

WHO representatives point out that AIDS may soon become problem number one, since so far there are no effective cures to fight it.

A well-known American scientist and anthropologist, in a letter to Editor, Patriot, analyses the history and background of the deadly AIDS which started in the US and has now spread to Europe. The writer, who wants to remain anonymous, has expressed the fear that India may face a danger from this disease in the near future.

forms and in most cases leads to death.

AIDS has recently been registered inasmany as 16 countries, primarily in those which import American blood donations. For some of the countries the disease has already become extremely dangerous.

The first signs of AIDS appeared in 1978 with an outburst of this disease in New York

among immigrants from Haiti. At that time, however, no one seemed to bother to pay any serious attention both on the part of the local authorities and the US public at large. In 1980 there was another sign of AIDS and again in New York. This time in addition to Haitian immigrants the disease struck local Americans, primarily drug addicts and homosexuals. By February 1983, AIDS had affected large sections of the American population and had been registered in 33 states. New York accounted for 49 per cent of all the cases that had been officially registered in the US by that time.

Concerned American citizens and organisations began to wonder why does AIDS, just like some other previously unknown diseases such as bizarre pneumonia or the so-called Legion- continued on page 7 col. 2

PATRIOT *

Disinformation about the origins of AIDS was spread by the Soviet disinformation office in the 1980s.

to develop new and dangerous biological weapons." This claim, that the US government had created AIDS, a devastating illness that was killing many people around the globe at this time, was false. The story was soon picked up by other Russian newspapers. The next year, a British tabloid published a version of the story as well. By 1987, the story had appeared in newspapers across at least fifty countries.

It was a big problem that this false story was spread. The Pentagon, of course, had not invented AIDS to be used as a weapon. But many people began to believe it anyway. In a study done decades later, 50 percent of a group of Americans surveyed believed that the story was true. The story had been spread by Soviet agents to create anger and suspicion toward the US government. While there was nothing credible about the story, it worked.

What Next?

Knowing that disinformation exists, and that it's pretty widespread, might be shocking and worrying. You may wonder if you've ever read something that was part of a disinformation campaign. You may wonder whether you believed it. The good news is that there are ways to recognize disinformation and to uncover the truth. Much of what we read may be written with a particular bias. It is very common to read articles and watch movies that have the same biases we do. But bias is different from disinformation. The best way to distinguish disinformation and fake news from biased information or serious journalism is to know what each looks like.

There are many great sources of information online, including major news outlets like this one. But not all information online is true, and disinformation can spread fast.

Characteristics of Disinformation

It can be hard to evaluate whether information you are reading online is accurate, or if it is part of a disinformation campaign. The problem with identifying disinformation is that it can take some time to do. For example, you might see something on Twitter that seems like it could be true, so you share it. Several days later, researchers show evidence that it isn't true. But you have already shared the tweet, and your friends have then shared it. As a result, the disinformation has spread rapidly across social media. Once disinformation is spread, the damage is already done. It is difficult for people to rethink and reevaluate something they already believe to be true. It is much easier to stop that belief in the first place.

With disinformation, it is challenging to find where it originated and just as difficult to prove the creator intended to spread false information. This, of course, is one of the key definitions of disinformation. Tracing back a piece of disinformation can be both difficult and time consuming.

The best way to stop the spread of disinformation is to learn to think critically about it from the first time you see it. If you think critically about disinformation and discover that a certain article or blog post doesn't make sense, or that it is not verifiable, then you can stop the spread of false information before it starts.

Learning to Live Critically

Use critical thinking skills when watching TV, going online, or reading.

The key to spotting disinformation is learning how to read critically. Discussions about reading news articles and social media posts with a critical eye are really about media literacy. "Literacy" means the ability to know how to read and write. In the past, "literacy" referred only to learning how to read the written word—typically in the form of books and printed articles. In the twenty-first century, though, media literacy is just as important as the traditional form of literacy. In fact, it's an essential skill that everyone should learn. According to the Media Literacy Project, "Media literacy is the ability to access, analyze, evaluate, and create media. Media literate youth and adults are better able to understand the complex messages we receive from television, radio, internet, newspapers, magazines, books, billboards, video games, music, and all other forms of media."

When teaching media literacy, media educator Elizabeth Thoman focuses on the following five main principles:

1. All media messages are constructed;
2. All media are constructed using their own set of rules;
3. Different people will have different reactions to the same media message;
4. Media are typically produced by businesses that want to earn money; and
5. Media have "embedded" values and points of view.

All Media Messages Are Constructed

Recognizing that media messages are constructed means that we understand that time, effort, multiple drafts, and varying perspectives are behind the final product that you see. If you are reading a newspaper article or looking at a billboard, a lot of time and effort went into creating it. It is likely that earlier drafts, sketches, and ideas were created and discarded. This is an important point. Because media is so carefully constructed, it has a purpose. Whether you

Advertisements are created by a group of experts who spend a lot of time and money to try to send a particular message.

are reading a blog post or watching an advertisement, try to think of what the purpose of that piece is.

All Media Are Constructed Using Their Own Sets of Rules

Different forms of media have different ways of communicating. For example, horror movies usually use creepy-sounding music to make audiences more afraid. Newspaper articles use headlines that will grab your attention. Radio-friendly music is usually produced not only so that it will be catchy but also so it will run just two to three minutes in length. (Otherwise, radio stations won't play it!) All of these different kinds of media have their own rules to follow. Understanding what these rules are will help you to better understand the purpose behind what you read or see.

Different People Will Have Different Reactions to the Same Media Message

As Thoman writes, "Because of each individual's age, upbringing and education, no two people see the same movie or hear the same song on the radio." We should be open to the fact that other people may understand what they read or watch in ways different to how we understand it. Asking questions about how different people encounter the media in different ways helps us to think more critically about media. Asking questions allows us to broaden our perspective.

Not everyone experiences media messages in the same way. That's why it is important to talk to different people about what you read and see.

Media Are Typically Produced by Businesses That Want to Earn Money

One of the most important things to remember is that businesses that create media (whether newspapers, production companies, or advertising companies) need

Media companies need money to stay in business.
They rely on advertising to make money.

to earn money to survive. These companies need money
to produce even more media. Their survival is based
on people liking their product and paying for it. For
example, newspaper editors typically lay out the pages of
their papers with ads before they lay out the news. The
remaining space is for news articles. Be aware that this
is a money-making process. Then think about how that
influences the media you are reading or watching.

An advertisement will not talk about any faults in
the product it is selling. Ads won't discuss flaws in any
other products made by the same company. This is why
newspapers have to disclose the companies that provide
their funding. Disclosures help readers judge whether or
not there is any conflict of interest. A conflict of interest
would be a situation in which, for example, to write an

accurate and truthful story, you would need to include negative information about the companies that pay you.

Media Have "Embedded" Values and Points of View

Everything that is conveyed in a media message is for a reason. Characters are developed and actors are picked. Stories are told in a particular way to spark interest. According to Thoman, "It is important to learn how to 'read' all kinds of media messages in order to discover the points of view that are embedded in them. Only then can we judge whether to accept or reject these messages as we negotiate our way each day through our mediated environment."

Thoman outlines several questions that everyone should ask themselves when reading media. They are:

> Who created this message and why are they sending it? What techniques are being used to attract my attention? What lifestyles, values, and points of view are represented in the message? How might different people understand this message differently from me? What is omitted from this message?

Overall, media literacy is about learning to ask questions about what we see or read. We should never take anything for face value. We should always question what we are reading or experiencing. This is the first step to combatting the spread of disinformation. If we can question what we are reading, then we might take more time to discover where it is coming from and why.

Learning Your ABCs

While learning media literacy is the first step in fighting false news, you can also take a more specific approach to disinformation. According to Ben Nimmo, a senior fellow at the Institute for Statecraft, the intent to spread false information can be uncovered using an "ABC" approach. This approach states that consumers should judge information based on three criteria: "the accuracy of factual statements, balance in reporting, and the credibility of sources chosen."

A Is for Accuracy

Accuracy in reporting means that the information is correct and generally unbiased. Accuracy is very important for serious journalists and reputable newspapers. In fact,

Chris Christie mistakenly gave false information during a presidential debate in 2015, but this was not an example of disinformation.

newspapers usually pay people to check and then double-check facts and details in reporting. This is especially important because sometimes incorrect information can be given not on purpose, but in error. For example, former New Jersey governor Chris Christie stated at a presidential debate in 2015: "When I stand across from King Hussein of Jordan, and I say to him, 'You have a friend again, sir, who will stand with you to fight this fight,' he'll change his mind."

The problem with this statement was that King Hussein of Jordan had died in 1999. Christie later apologized and stated that he misspoke. The truth was easily verifiable from multiple sources. We can imagine that this was a mistake and was not a part of a campaign to deliberately mislead. This means that Christie's error was one of misinformation. It was not a deliberate attempt to spread false information, meaning it was not disinformation.

B Is for Balance

Balance in reporting is also a way to check whether or not your information is correct. When scanning headlines on Facebook or Twitter, it is important to judge whether or not the headline reads in a biased or unbiased way. News reporting is supposed to be impartial. This means that the facts are reported alone without inserting the reporter's opinion. However, there are more and more "news" outlets that publish opinion pieces, rather than reported pieces.

Opinion pieces might get more attention because they can be sensationalist. Something that is sensationalist will get a lot of clicks or views, even though this is done at the expense of accuracy. Usually it is easy to see this by simply reading the headline of a news article. A biased, sensationalist headline might read something like, "Racist Groups Savagely Attack Peaceful Protesters." Notice that in this headline there are adjectives like "peaceful" and adverbs like "savagely." Adjectives and adverbs are used for description and are often used to persuade, rather than to report. A headline that reads in a more unbiased way, written about the same event, might say simply, "Protest Ends in Violence." Unbiased articles seek to report the facts, rather than to persuade readers.

To check balance, it is also important to note the sources of the articles you are reading. Are both sides of a controversy given the chance to speak? Are experts who give their opinions on a topic connected to any interests that make their opinions more biased? For example, a 2016 article published in *China People's Daily* detailed how a US warship came very close to the South China Sea Islands. The reporter interviewed a panel of experts for so-called unbiased opinions on whether this US warship had violated China's territorial waters. The experts all stated that the US had and was in the wrong. However, looking at the profiles of the experts featured in the article, all four of them worked for the Chinese government. Thus, their opinions likely were biased in favor of the Chinese government.

It would have been relatively easy for the journalist who wrote the article to reach out to the US government

A US warship comes close to the South China Sea Islands. An unbalanced article about the approach of a US ship was published in *China People's Daily*.

and ask for a statement from US officials. In fact, the US stance on territorial claims in the South China Sea was published online on US government websites. All the reporter had to do was to look up this information and include it in the article. Because the reporter did not try for a balanced report of what happened, this example was likely one of disinformation.

C Is for Credibility

Finally, it may be easier to discover disinformation if an article uses sources who are not credible experts on the topic when there are credible experts that are available to be interviewed. For example, if a journalist is writing on complex details about the economy, but only interviews politicians and no economists, that suggests the

WHAT'S FREEDOM OF SPEECH GOT TO DO WITH IT?

Freedom of speech and of the press is an important pillar in free and democratic nations. It was established in the First Amendment of the US Constitution and Article 19 of the Universal Declaration of Human Rights, which is a document drafted by the United Nations (UN). That's why some governments have struggled with writing and passing laws against spreading disinformation. While disinformation is harmful, laws against disinformation could lead to censorship and even violating human rights.

In early 2018, Germany instituted its first law against fake news. France was considering a similar law. But there have been many critics who have spoken out against these laws. Critics ask, for example, who gets to determine what is fake news and how do they determine that? An editorial in the French newspaper *Le Monde* stated that a law "on a subject as crucial as the freedom of the press, is by nature dangerous." Many declare that the best way to combat disinformation is not through laws but through education instead.

information in the article is not credible. Credible sources are experts in their topic and are usually well-known in their field. When determining whether or not a post or an article is trustworthy, it is important to pay attention to the sources used and to evaluate whether or not they are credible. You can even do a quick Google search to find out more about the sources used in a news article. If you can't find anything about them, that might be a sign that you shouldn't trust what they were quoted as saying.

This system can be very useful to help you evaluate articles or posts to determine if they are part of a disinformation campaign. However, as Nimmo states, "Care and judgment must be exercised in the use of this ABC [system]: mistakes do happen, editors make errors of judgment and politicians fumble their lines ... If a speaker or a news outlet violates the ABC principles repeatedly, and does not correct their errors, they should be considered as committing disinformation." What this means is that errors can be made, which doesn't mean that they were done purposefully. Watch to see if errors occur again and again and are not corrected. This might be yet another sign that both the information being published—and the intentions of the publisher—should not be trusted.

The Nitty-Gritty of Disinformation

The above categories can help you detect disinformation based on the content of what you read. But there's another way to spot disinformation—by following how it is spread. In May 2017, data scientist Kris Shaffer analyzed an organized disinformation campaign. This campaign attempted to sway the French presidential elections for the far-right nationalist candidate Marine Le Pen. He found that disinformation was spread in very predictable ways.

First, an anonymous user would "dump" information on a particular page where followers were more likely to have extremist views. Next, a small number of "catalyst" accounts would access that information and bring it to more mainstream sites, like Twitter or Facebook. Then, automated accounts and regular users who thought the information they were sharing was true would share this information until it reached a larger audience and a more mainstream platform. Eventually, a celebrity or a person with a wide social media following would share the post. Finally, it would get picked up by some mainstream news sources. At this point, the false news would be widely spread, attracting a large following of people who believed it to be true.

Bots, Bots, and More Bots

In studying how the spread of this disinformation occurred, Shaffer noted that "catalysts and amplifiers [are used] to bring propaganda to the attention of the public at large, with the goal of getting a major influencer outside your community to boost it into mainstream media or campaign activities." What are catalysts and amplifiers? Oftentimes, these are bots that are set up particularly to circulate information. Bots are automated accounts

NOT YOUR AVERAGE SOCK PUPPET

A sock puppet account is similar to a bot. It is an account created by someone to appear as if it were controlled by another person. For example, a man named Joe Smith might make an account that appears as if it is owned by popular singer Carrie Underwood. In the world of digital media, Carrie Underwood would be what's called an "influencer." An influencer is someone who has a big social media presence and lots of fans or followers who will be reading anything and everything he or she posts. Influencers are important components of disinformation campaigns. If Joe Smith were able to get fans of Carrie Underwood to follow the sock puppet account, even though it is not her real account, he would attract a lot of followers. And if he wanted to spread false information rapidly, he could then draw on these fans and followers to retweet or repost whatever he posts on the page.

that are controlled by code that has been written by a human user. Sometimes these bots are set up for fun. Yet oftentimes they are set up for deceptive reasons. They can be set up to impersonate a real person, or to spread disinformation. What they do is circulate information before it is picked up by a wider audience. They are, in some cases, the first step in spreading disinformation.

Bots act as signal boosters. What this means is that they use a wider social media following to spread false information quicker than they would otherwise be able to do. The spread of information online is all about influence and audience. You might have something very important to say. However, if you only have a handful of followers, it might be hard to get your message out. On the other hand, someone who wants to make a silly joke might see that joke spread all over the internet if they have enough followers.

So how can you pick out whether or not the information you are reading has come from a bot or a bot-like account? There are several things that they have in common. First of all, check to see how often information is being posted. If you are following a user on Twitter and posts are made continuously throughout the day and night with only short breaks in between them, it is highly likely that the account is automated.

On Twitter, it is also somewhat easy to recognize a retweet bot. These bots retweet posts from catalyst accounts, or accounts that contain certain keywords. These automated accounts are coded so that if they come across a certain word or words in an account, they automatically retweet it. If you see a Twitter account that is exclusively composed of retweets, check to make sure it isn't a tweet bot. Of course, not all accounts that spread disinformation are automated. Some accounts that spread disinformation do so unintentionally, while others are people (and not bots) who spread information manually.

Another tactic that those who spread disinformation use is to steal information from other accounts. These people may follow an account that often posts clickbait material. Then they will report on that material, with the same headline, while substituting the link that was originally given with a link to their own material.

As Shaffer states,

> The creators [of such bots] are not politically motivated. They're simply trying to get ad revenue by tricking people into clicking on their link. But because most click-bait content is also often the most polarizing content, these bots end up amplifying polarizing content that is sometimes itself misinformation or disinformation. This subtly contributes to the increased polarization in our culture, and when it overlaps with another influence operation, can end up amplifying the effects of that influence operation."

Of course, identifying disinformation and how it is spread is only half of the equation. Luckily, there are many ways to combat disinformation.

A lawyer for Facebook, Colin
Stretch, testifies about
Russian disinformation in
front of Congress in 2017.

Mr. Colin Stretch

Fighting Disinformation

Once you've identified disinformation, it is important to try to take action to stop its spread. This can be done in multiple ways. While you can play an important role in stopping the spread of disinformation, by the time you see it, many other people have probably seen it too. That means that it is especially important that media companies and governments also work to stop the spread of disinformation—even before it starts.

Governments Step Up

In 2016, the European Parliament took its first steps to combat disinformation. The European Parliament recognized that the spread of disinformation was a problem, particularly in terms of disinformation spread purposefully by the Russian government against the European Union. Europe began steps to impose fines on media companies that republished disinformation. Some countries also took further steps. The Czech Republic, for example, created a task force whose responsibility was information security. It was the task force's job to hunt down how disinformation campaigns began and to try to prevent these campaigns from inflicting any damage.

Another important step that governments can take is to inform their citizens about disinformation. According to a research center called the Warsaw Institute, there are many organizations that "engage in the policy of revealing false information, simultaneously juxtaposing it with facts." This means that these organizations will

The European Parliament, shown here, has recognized the importance of combatting disinformation.

uncover false information and then show how that information is wrong by giving the accurate facts and statistics. Government initiatives such as StopFake publish brochures on disinformation. They also publish brochures that contradict false claims. The Integrity Initiative of the Institute for Statecraft in the United Kingdom works to collect information on the spread of propaganda and disinformation. The French CrossCheck project also works on informing people of the truth in the face of disinformation campaigns.

However, there are also some drawbacks to when governments get involved in stopping the spread of disinformation. In some countries around the world, journalists are restricted by their governments. Sometimes these governments institute laws that restrict freedom of speech and freedom of the press for their own benefit. There are even instances where journalists who report information the government doesn't like are threatened. It's a slippery slope from saying that fake news is illegal to saying that news that does not reflect well on the government is illegal. For example, a bill was introduced in the Philippines in 2017 to stop fake news by imposing a prison sentence of five years on anyone who was caught spreading it. However, the bill stated that fake news could include anything that causes "panic, division, chaos, violence, and hate, or those which exhibit a propaganda to black or discredit one's reputation." This definition is very broad. Critics fear that it could be used to imprison anyone who speaks or writes critically about the government in the Philippines.

Newspapers:
It's OK to Say I'm Sorry

The news industry also has a role to play in stopping disinformation. In addition to providing serious journalism, newspapers and news sources should be careful to fact-check everything before publication. If they publish any error, they should be quick to correct it.

There are some online news organizations that operate as fact-checkers themselves, including PolitiFact and Factcheck.org. A simple search on one of these websites can pull up the researched and compiled facts about a particular topic. Some newspapers, like the *Guardian*, have even drawn on crowdsourcing to verify documents and determine what is newsworthy.

Websites like PolitiFact can help readers fact-check information they come across.

Tech Solutions

In many ways, technology companies are at the forefront of combatting disinformation. After uncovering the extent of disinformation spread on Facebook, for example, the company took major steps to prevent its platform from being used in that way again. In 2017, Facebook launched a new tool through its "Help Center" that can inform users as to whether or not they followed an account or liked a post that spread disinformation related to the 2016 US presidential elections. The company also announced that it would suspend or delete accounts that spread such disinformation, after identifying them through special algorithms, or codes, that the company developed. Several social media companies have also added "disputed news" tags to their platform that appear if fake news is shared.

Many critics have argued that other social media companies should also create ways to automatically identify fake news. Computer scientists like Eugenio Tacchini are currently working on such tools. Using a database of 15,500 Facebook posts and nearly 1 million users, Tacchini and his colleagues were able to use their automatic fake news detection tool to find fake news with an accuracy rate of 99 percent.

Finally, technology and social media companies can make it harder for people to create false online accounts. Many experts have suggested that social media companies use "real name registration." This allows users to register for an account only once their identification has been verified. Real name registration would put an end to bot

Your Privacy
Staying Safe
Keeping Your Account Secure
Unfriending or Blocking
Someone
Hacked and Fake Accounts

Hacked and Fake Accounts

Your account should represent you, and only you should have access to your account. If someone gains access to your account, or creates an account to pretend to be you or someone else, we want to help. We also encourage you to let us know about accounts that represent fake or fictional people, pets, celebrities or organizations.

Hacked Accounts

I think my account was hacked or someone is using it without my permission.

I think my friend's account was hacked.

Impersonation Accounts

How do I report an account for impersonation?

How do I report an account that's pretending to be me?

How do I request information about a timeline that was impersonating me?

Fake Accounts

How do I report a fake account?

Some media experts want people to register for online accounts using only their real name. This would cut down on the number of fake accounts on the web.

accounts and stolen accounts, which are often used to spread disinformation.

Disinformation Tools

For individuals who want to combat disinformation themselves, there are a lot of resources available. In the United States, First Draft, a project of the Harvard Kennedy School Shorenstein Center, provides videos and information checklists, online training in information verification for journalists, and more resources to combat misinformation and disinformation campaigns. Their resources include guides to photo and video verification. The Visual Verification Guide asks readers to ask themselves several questions, including: "Are you looking at the original version?" "Do you know who captured

FACEBOOK'S FLAGGING SYSTEM

In December 2016, Facebook rolled out a new tool allowing users to "flag" disputed information. However, a year later, this tool was dropped from the platform. That's because research conducted by Facebook showed that it did not stop users from spreading fake news online. In fact, this research showed that "putting a strong image, like a red flag, next to an article may actually [encourage] deeply held beliefs—the opposite effect to what we intended," according to Tessa Lyons at Facebook.

Instead, Facebook will show related fact-checked articles that dispute the claims of the false post next to it. Then, if a user clicks to share a fake news story, a pop-up will appear with links to those fact-checked sources. The pop-up will ask if the user still wants to post the article. Early research suggests that while this new tool doesn't stop people from reading the articles, it does lower the amount of users who will share them.

But critics of Facebook's policies in regard to disinformation don't think this will be enough. Tim Luckhurst, a professor of journalism at the University of Kent, states, "We have a generation of people that are so ... skeptical of evidence-based news, we need [government] regulation [instead of warnings]."

the photo?" and "Do you know where the photo was captured?" Based on your answers to these questions, you are given a green, red, or yellow/orange color signaling the level of verification you have achieved.

For example, let's say there is a controversial image that is being shared by your friends on social media. You want to check and make sure that this image is real before you share it yourself. First Draft suggests that you first do a reverse Google image search at https://reverse.photos to search for other places the image was published.

If you find identical copies of the image published online before the supposed event took place, then you are most likely looking at an image that was taken out of its original context. This would get a red light in First Draft's guide. However, if you are a journalist and can say the image "was sent to us directly and we have spoken to the source," then you can verify the photo. This would receive a green light from the guide. For regular social media users and non-journalists, the response instead could be "We are unable to find other versions online and basic ... checks suggest that it has not been manipulated." This response provides a reasonable amount of confidence that this is the original photo, although it cannot be fully verified. This would receive a yellow light from First Draft's guide.

It's important to note that it is rare to fully verify photos and videos on the internet, although they can be verified with a reasonable amount of certainty. First Draft's verification guides have also been made into a free extension for Google Chrome browsers. When you open up an image or a video in your browser, this extension will run you through the checklist to verify the image. It will then give you a score based on the information you input.

Verification Junkie is another website that can help online users navigate through disinformation. Managed by Josh Stearns, the website is an inventory of tools that can be used to verify and fact-check online content. One of the tools profiled on the site, Emergent.Info, is noted to be "a real-time rumor tracker … that aims to develop best practices for debunking misinformation." Rumors tracked on Emergent.Info range from "There will be a *Sons of Anarchy* film," which was determined to be false, to "Jordan's King Abdullah II will participate in air strikes against ISIS," which was also determined to be false.

What Can You Do?

All of these tools are useful for identifying disinformation, but what can you do once you've identified it? The first thing to do is to report what you've found as fake news. On Facebook you can do this by clicking the upper right-hand corner of a post, selecting "Report post," then "I think it shouldn't be on Facebook," and finally, "It's a false news story." Facebook will then investigate the post. If they determine that it is false information, they will take it down and potentially block the user.

If you find websites that are distributing disinformation near the top of a Google search, you can also report this by clicking on "feedback" at the bottom of the Google search page. Then you'll write what you've found, while providing a link. You can also report fake news on platforms like Twitter and Instagram. Report wrong

YOU AND YOUR DATA

Every time you open your browser and go online, your browsing history, location data, purchasing patterns, and some personal information is logged. Within seconds, that information can be shared with dozens of online firms. This information is then combined with other information about you, including your past history online, and even your phone number and email address, and sold to digital advertising companies and other data collection companies. What does this have to do with disinformation? The same data collection that is being sent to advertising companies to sell you products is also being used by "disinformation operators."

Disinformation operators use this data to experiment with how to spread fake messages. Armed with users' personal data, they can track when certain groups of people are more likely to read an article and to find it on a Google search, or even how to tailor their headlines to make them more likely to be read. Basically, when disinformation operatives get users' data, they can use them as guinea pigs to test their disinformation campaigns. Critics state that this is one reason why digital privacy regulations are more important now than ever before.

information to newspapers by emailing authors or editors or using online contact forms on the website. (Of course you should always ask the permission of a trusted adult before logging on to social media sites or sending emails.)

Both reputable and "fake" news companies rely on their readers to survive—this means that regular people have a lot of power. If you see a particular website or newspaper that is publishing disinformation or fake news, don't read it anymore. Tell your friends about what you've discovered and tell them not to share or frequent those posts or websites anymore either. If you notice advertisers on a website that publishes fake news, you can contact them and tell them how dissatisfied you are to see their product associated with such a website. On the other hand, support real, serious journalism. If there are newspapers you like that only publish trustworthy information, read them. If you can, buy a subscription to them. You can also ask your parents to support their preferred newspaper by buying a subscription. If you're on social media, think before sharing. And, above all, think deeply about the information that you are exposed to— whether online, on TV, or elsewhere.

Presidential candidates Hillary Clinton and Donald Trump debate in 2016. Russian disinformation was used to influence the 2016 US presidential election.

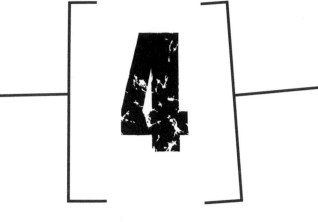

Putting Your Skills into Action

n late 2016, the word "disinformation" became a popular term across American news media. This was because of reports that Russia had engaged in a campaign of disinformation in order to sway the US presidential election that year in favor of Republican candidate Donald Trump against Democratic candidate Hillary Clinton.

Understanding Russia's Disinformation Campaign

Ever since the breakup of the Soviet Union, Russia has increasingly used disinformation as a military strategy. (The US government has also engaged in disinformation campaigns, which became more widespread in the 1980s and 1990s.) Russian disinformation became so widespread that the European Union and NATO both set up special units to address and disprove false information released by Russia.

This came to a head with the US presidential election in 2016. In the lead-up to the election, the US intelligence community shared information that the Russians had hacked the servers of the Democratic National Commitee (DNC) and political figures aligned with Hillary Clinton's campaign. Russian agents leaked these emails to the website WikiLeaks, which then published them. The Russian government denied this accusation, although there was evidence that proved that they were involved. In December 2016, senior intelligence officers testified that they believed that Vladimir Putin, the president of Russia, directed the disinformation campaign himself. The officers stated that it had begun as a way to attack Hillary Clinton and destabilize the United States' position in the global economy. Ultimately, the purpose was to aid Donald Trump in the election. The Russian government believed that he would be friendlier toward Russian interests.

Definitive Proof

In January 2017, the Office of the Director of National Intelligence (DNI) published the following statement:

> President Vladimir Putin ordered an influence campaign in 2016 aimed at the US presidential election. Russia's goals were to undermine public

faith in the US democratic process, denigrate Secretary Clinton, and harm her electability and potential presidency. We further assess Putin and the Russian Government developed a clear preference for President-elect Trump. We have high confidence in these judgments.

US intelligence officials believe that Russian president Vladimir Putin was involved in the Russian disinformation campaign.

While hacking political groups in the United States, the Russian government also set its sights on spreading disinformation on social media. According to testimony given by Facebook in November 2017, approximately 126 million users in the United States saw posts that had been created by Russian government–affiliated accounts that spread disinformation. Google testified that it discovered many ads that had been created by individuals with Russian ties. It also stated that more than one thousand YouTube videos were posted as part of the disinformation campaign. Twitter executives testified that more than 2,700 accounts were tied to the Internet Research Agency, a Russian-sponsored organization tasked with spreading disinformation.

The Internet Research Agency began by gathering American followers on social media around issues like religion and immigration. Then they bought political ads to spread their messages. Finally, they used their social media followers to organize political rallies across the United States.

In September 2017, Facebook stated that roughly three thousand political ads that attempted to persuade Americans to vote for a particular candidate in the 2016 US presidential elections were bought by accounts that were run out of Russia. These ads targeted people who lived in certain areas of the United States, where that candidate needed votes. The advertisements that these particular groups of people were shown used false claims and disinformation to spread lies about the other candidate. While announcing the extent of the disinformation campaign, Facebook admitted that disinformation was a growing problem that the company was going to work to fix.

Holding Companies Responsible

For many people, Facebook's response was not enough. Jonathan Albright, research director at Columbia University's Tow Center for Digital Journalism, stated, "Facebook built incredibly effective tools which let

UNILEVER FOR THE WIN!

In February 2018, the multinational corporation Unilever made headlines. The company announced that it would pull its advertisements from companies like Facebook and Google if they didn't find a way to stop the spread of fake news on their sites. Unilever spends approximately $2 billion each year on advertisements. This translates to a lot of lost money for digital companies if Unilever doesn't place its ads with them.

"Unilever, as a trusted advertiser does not want to advertise on platforms which do not make a positive contribution to society," Keith Weed, the CMO of Unilever, stated. "Fake news, racism, sexism, terrorists spreading messages of hate, toxic content directed at children—parts of the internet we have ended up with is a

Unilever CMO Keith Weed has spoken out about disinformation and negative media messages.

million miles from where we thought it would take us. It is in the digital media industry's interest to listen and act on this. Before viewers stop viewing, advertisers stop advertising and publishers stop publishing."

Russia profile citizens here in the US and figure out to manipulate us. Facebook, essentially, gave them everything they needed."

Roger McNamee, who had invested early in Facebook, stated, "In its heyday, television brought the country together, giving viewers a shared set of facts and experiences. Facebook does just the opposite, enabling every user to have a unique set of facts, driving the country apart for profit."

Media Literacy in Action

In June 2016, a man named Melvin Redick used his Facebook page to post the following message: "These guys show hidden truth about Hillary Clinton, George Soros and other leaders of the US. Visit #DCLeaks

The DCLeaks website was used by Russian hackers as part of their disinformation campaign.

website. It's really interesting!" This was one of the first messages posted about a new website, DCLeaks, that had been launched only several days earlier. The DCLeaks site posted material stolen by Russian hackers from the Democratic Committee.

If you saw that message in an online group, how would you investigate it before sharing it? You could do a search for Melvin Redick on Facebook and see if he posted anything else, or if this was his only post. You could even do a quick Google search for his name to see if it popped up anywhere. If you visited the DCLeaks website, you could look for information about when it was published online, either by Googling the web address or checking for posting dates on the website. You could also explore the content of what was being posted. The word "leak" suggests information that it is illegally shared. This might make you suspicious of the motives of the leakers. You could also search the website for inflammatory and biased writing. Are politicians called "liars" or "thieves" without any information to back up these descriptions? Does the website state how it received the information it is publishing?

Investigators later looked into Melvin Redick's post and the DCLeaks website. They discovered that there was no record of Melvin Redick in the hometown he listed on his profile. Investigators also saw Redick's profile picture had been stolen from another Facebook account. When they researched the DCLeaks website, they eventually discovered that it had been launched by a Russian military intelligence agency.

SAYING SORRY

Mark Zuckerberg, the CEO of Facebook, has received a lot of criticism because of how easily disinformation spreads on Facebook. In the immediate aftermath of the US presidential election in 2016, Zuckerberg stated that he did not believe that there had been any disinformation spread on Facebook about the election. Later, after the extent of the disinformation campaign came to light, Zuckerberg issued the following statement:

After the election, I made a comment that I thought the idea misinformation on Facebook changed the outcome of the election was a crazy idea. Calling that crazy was dismissive and I regret it. This is too important an issue to be dismissive ... We will continue to work to build a community for all people. We will do our part to defend against nation states attempting to spread misinformation and subvert elections. We'll keep working to ensure the integrity of free and fair elections around the world, and to ensure our community is a platform for all ideas and force for good in democracy.

This photoshopped image of comedian Aziz Ansari was spread across social media by Russian intelligence officials.

Russian intelligence agents also shared photoshopped images on social media to trick people. For example, before the election in November 2016, some accounts started to share a picture of the comedian Aziz Ansari on Twitter. In this photo, Ansari holds up a sign. On the sign is written "Save time. Avoid the line. Vote from home. Tweet ClintonKaine with the hashtag #PresidentialElection on November 8th, 2016 between 8AM and 6PM to cast your vote."

The image seems to suggest that people can vote in the presidential elections just by tweeting the candidate they are voting for. To check and see if this was true, you could do a Google search using terms like "tweet,"

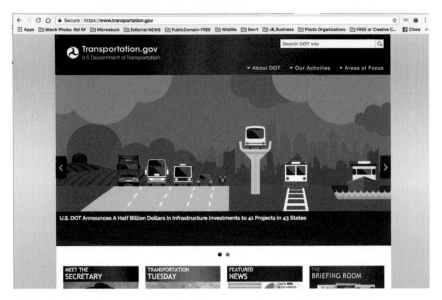

Official government websites can be used to confirm information that you read online and are reliable sources of information.

"voting," and "US presidential elections." If you didn't find any confirmation that you could vote by tweeting on governmental websites (websites that end with .gov instead of .com) then you could assume that this wasn't true. You could also do a reverse image search to see if this image appeared anywhere else in a different version. If you entered in the link with the image, you would find that the image was circulated long before the election. However, the writing on the sign Ansari held was different. While it was a real photograph of Aziz Ansari, it had been photoshopped to change what had been written on the sign.

Obviously, the point of that image was to deliberately mislead people into thinking that they could vote via Twitter. This would mean that their votes wouldn't be counted. Although this piece of disinformation was uncovered, experts have not been able to say how many people believed it and did not officially vote because of it.

Dangerous Disinformation

The examples above show how dangerous disinformation can be—and also how easy it can be to find fake news with a few targeted searches. What we read in the news shapes our worldview and helps us to develop our own opinions. The consequences if we are tricked into believing false news are great. In the case of the 2016 US presidential election, disinformation most likely changed the course of the election. Now that we know more about the extent of disinformation out there, it is our job to become media literate, to investigate claims we read before sharing them, and, above all, to think critically about the world around us.

Digital media is an important part of our lives, so we must always approach media messages critically.

GLOSSARY

amplifiers Online accounts that are used to spread disinformation by sharing it widely on social media platforms.

bias Prejudicial feelings for or against something.

bot An online, coded program that can work without a person or user directing it.

campaign An organized plan to achieve a goal.

catalyst A person or thing that starts an event; in the case of disinformation, accounts that first spread false news.

censorship Blocking the spread of information or artistic works that are considered obscene, politically incorrect, or harmful to the government.

clickbait Online articles, blogs, or other posts that attempt to get a large amount of viewers to click on the link to their website.

cynicism The habit of not believing what you hear or read.

disinformation False information that is intended to mislead.

extent The area covered by something or the degree to which something has spread.

fake news False information that appears to be news that is spread on the internet.

influencer A person who has the power to sway many people; particularly people who have a lot of followers online.

misinformation False information.

polarizing Causing people to become divided over an issue.

propaganda Biased information that is spread to get people to believe a certain political cause.

sensationalist Presenting stories in a shocking way so that people become Interested, even if it is not entirely accurate.

subvert To undermine or weaken the power of something.

verified Something that has been shown to be true.

FURTHER INFORMATION

Books

Anniss, Matt. *Cyber Wars*. I Witness War. New York: Cavendish Square, 2018.

Gerber, Larry. *The Distortion of Facts in the Digital Age*. Digital and Information Literacy. New York: Rosen Central, 2013.

Mara, Wil. *Fake News*. Ann Arbor, MI: Cherry Lake Publishing, 2018.

Websites

The British Library Board: Learning Disinformation
http://www.bl.uk/learning/cult/disinfo/disinformation.html

This interactive educational website includes a movie about disinformation and related activities.

National Geographic Kids: Spotting Fake News
https://kids.nationalgeographic.com/explore/ngk-sneak-peek/april-2017/fake-news

This National Geographic site teaches students how to determine if news is real or fake and provides five sample stories for students to test their new skills.

Videos

How False News Can Spread by Noah Tavlin
https://www.youtube.com/watch?v=cSKGa_7XJkg

This animated TED Ed talk by Noah Tavlin explores how disinformation spreads.

How to Spot Fake News (And Teach Kids to Be Media Savvy)
https://www.commonsensemedia.org/blog/how-to-spot-fake-news-and-teach-kids-to-be-media-savvy

This video by Common Sense Media gives tips on how to spot fake news.

BIBLIOGRAPHY

BBC. "Facebook Ditches Fake News Warning Flag."
December 21, 2017. http://www.bbc.com/news/
technology-42438750.

Frenkel, Sheera, and Katie Benner. "To Stir Discord in
2016, Russians Turned Most Often to Facebook." *New
York Times*, February 17, 2018. https://www.nytimes.
com/2018/02/17/technology/indictment-russian-tech-
facebook.html.

Ghosh, Dipayan, and Ben Scott. "Disinformation Is
Becoming Unstoppable." *Time*, January 24, 2018.
http://time.com/5112847/facebook-fake-news-
unstoppable.

Jackson, Dean. "Issue Brief: Distinguishing Disinformation
from Propaganda, Misinformation, and 'Fake News'."
National Endowment for Democracy, October 17,
2017. https://www.ned.org/issue-brief-distinguishing-
disinformation-from-propaganda-misinformation-and-
fake-news.

Levin, Sam. "Mark Zuckerberg: I Regret Ridiculing
Fears Over Facebook's Effect on Election." *Guardian*,
September 27, 2017. https://www.theguardian.com/
technology/2017/sep/27/mark-zuckerberg-facebook-
2016-election-fake-news.

Modell, Josh. "Russian Hackers Used a Secret Weapon: Aziz Ansari." *AVClub*, November 2, 2017. https://www. avclub.com/russian-hackers-used-a-secret-weapon-aziz-ansari-1820076677.

Thoman, Elizabeth. "Skills and Strategies for Media Education." Center for Media Literacy. Retrieved March 1, 2018. http://www.medialit.org/reading-room/skills-strategies-media-education.

Wagner, Kurt. "These are Some of the Tweets and Facebook Ads Russia Used to Try and Influence the 2016 Presidential Election." *Recode*, October 31, 2017. https://www.recode.net/2017/10/31/16587174/fake-ads-news-propaganda-congress-facebook-twitter-google-tech-hearing.

Weed, Keith. "Unilever Will Not Invest in Online Platforms that Create Division." Unilever, December 2, 2018. https://www.unilever.com/news/Press-releases/2018/unilever-will-not-invest-in-online-platforms-that-create-division.html.

Wendling, Mike. "BBC Trending: Solutions That Can Stop Fake News Spreading." *BBC News*, January 30, 2017. http://www.bbc.com/news/blogs-trending-38769996.

Zielinska, Maria. "In the Age of Post-Truth: Best Practices in Fighting Disinformation." Warsaw Institute Review, July 25, 2017. https://warsawinstitute.org/pl/age-post-truth-best-practices-fighting-disinformation.

INDEX

ABOUT THE AUTHOR

Elizabeth Schmermund is an author of educational books for young readers. She is also a news addict and professor and enjoys teaching her students how to sniff out seriously reported journalism.